MW01538018

Original title:

The Lynx's Frost

Author: Liisi Lendorav

ISBN HARDBACK: 978-9908-52-764-2

ISBN PAPERBACK: 978-9908-52-765-9

ISBN EBOOK: 978-9908-52-766-6

Caverns of Crystal Dreams

In caverns bright with shining gleams,
Where laughter flows like sparkling streams,
The air is thick with joy and light,
As spirits dance in sheer delight.

Each corner glows with splendor rare,
A symphony of love and care,
With twinkling stars above so near,
Unfolding tales that we hold dear.

The echoes sing of hearts entwined,
A universe of dreams designed,
In every whisper, cheer, and sigh,
We celebrate the night on high.

Night's Caress on Frosted Furs

Beneath the moon's soft silver rays,
The world is wrapped in glorious haze,
Frosted furs make shadows gleam,
A quiet hush, a midnight dream.

The air is filled with laughter's sound,
As friends in warmth and joy abound,
With tales of yore and hopes anew,
A tapestry of hearts so true.

The starlit sky, a canvas bright,
Paints every moment pure delight,
We bask beneath the cosmic hue,
With every star, our spirits flew.

Whispers of the Winter Night

The winter night, a wondrous sight,
With gentle whispers pure and bright,
Each flake that falls, a sparkling song,
Inviting all to join along.

The fireplace crackles, warmth embraced,
In every heart, joy is interlaced,
With mugs of cheer and tales of old,
The night unfolds like threads of gold.

Outside the windows, frost does weave,
A tapestry we can't believe,
So let us gather, sing, and play,
In whispers of this festive day.

Eyes in the Chilling Shadows

In chilling shadows, laughter flies,
With twinkles bright in all our eyes,
The night is young, the world aglow,
As joy and mirth fully bestow.

Around the fire, in stories spun,
Our hearts unite, our lives as one,
The dance of light and flickering flame,
In every breath, we call your name.

Underneath the blanket's embrace,
We find the warmth in every space,
With whispered dreams and soft caress,
In chilling shadows, we are blessed.

Enigma of the Winter Wilderness

In the stillness, the snowflakes fall,
A dance of white, enchanting all.
Twinkling stars break the night,
Whispers echo in pure delight.

Joyous laughter fills the air,
Children playing without a care.
Warmth of fires, bright and bold,
Stories of magic and winter unfold.

Trees adorned in glistening ice,
Nature's beauty, a paradise.
Footprints lead to dreams anew,
In this wilderness, life feels true.

The Icebound Watcher

Silent guardian of the night,
With frozen breath, shines so bright.
The moon whispers through frosty trees,
Beneath its gaze, all hearts feel ease.

A shimmering edge to every glance,
In snow's embrace, we find our dance.
The joy of gathering, friends unite,
Together sharing warmth and light.

Each sparkle tells a tale so grand,
Of winter's touch upon the land.
The Icebound Watcher, calm and wise,
Watches o'er the joyful skies.

Lurking Beneath the Snow

Hidden wonders beneath the white,
A world alive, a pure delight.
Creatures stir in quiet play,
As winter wraps the earth away.

Frosty breath in the crisp night air,
Brewing magic everywhere.
Laughter rings through frosted trees,
Bringing warmth, hearts feel at ease.

With every flake, a story told,
Of friendships forged, and hearts bold.
Under blankets, snug and tight,
A festive glow within the night.

Frosted Whispers of the Wild

Frosted whispers, soft and low,
Wander through the winter's glow.
In the woods where shadows play,
Magic awakens in a new way.

Sparkling trails of icy dreams,
Through crystalline woods, laughter beams.
Each moment etched on a frosty breath,
Celebrating life, conquering death.

A tapestry of silver and blue,
Threads of joy weave, a festive hue.
In nature's heart, we find our cheer,
With every snowflake, love draws near.

Secrets of the Frosted Fur

In the glimmering light, secrets dance,
Frosted fur shimmers, a thrilling chance.
Bursts of laughter in the crisp, cool air,
Joyful whispers float, swirl everywhere.

Gathered around, friends share delight,
With tales of old, beneath the starry night.
Hot cocoa flows, like a bubbling stream,
In the heart of winter, we chase our dream.

Nightfall in a Frozen Realm

When nightfall invites the silvery glow,
Crystals twinkle gently, secrets they know.
The moon casts shadows on the blanket of white,
As laughter rings out, pure magic ignites.

In the realm of frost, we dance with glee,
Warming our hearts, wild and free.
Tales of wonder by the fire's embrace,
In this frozen haven, we find our place.

Dreams Woven in Snowflakes

Each snowflake a wish, falling from skies,
Whirling like memories, a sweet surprise.
Huddled together, we joyously scheme,
Crafting our stories, wrapped snug in a dream.

The crisp winter air sings a delightful tune,
As we twirl and spin, under the moon.
Adventures await, in the snow-covered sea,
Where laughter and warmth blossom like a tree.

The Prowl of Diamond Whispers

Beneath the twilight, whispers take flight,
Diamonds of frost shimmer, pure and bright.
In the hush of the night, our hearts intertwine,
As the magic unfolds, we sip on moonshine.

Footprints in snow, our adventures begin,
Wandering freely, with cozy grins.
Echoes of cheer in the frosty embrace,
We share in the warmth of this sacred place.

Beneath the Swaying Snowy Branches

Under branches brushed with white,
Laughter dances, pure delight.
Twinkling lights in frosty air,
Joyful hearts, a lively affair.

Glistening crystals, nature's crown,
Children play, their spirits drown.
With every snowflake's gentle kiss,
We find warmth in winter's bliss.

Friends gather 'round the fire's glow,
Tales and songs, spirits flow.
Cups of cocoa, marshmallows sweet,
In this season, life feels complete.

So let us cherish this festive time,
With every laugh, the bells will chime.
Beneath the sway of snowy trees,
Together, we savor winter's breeze.

Night's Embrace in the Frigid Woodlands

The moonlit path through frost of night,
Whispers secrets, a magical sight.
Stars above, like diamonds bright,
Guiding dreams in the pale moonlight.

Snowflakes fall, a gentle dance,
Inviting all to take a chance.
In the cold, our laughter rings,
Celebrating all that winter brings.

Fires crackle, stories unfold,
Warmth surrounds, as hearts grow bold.
Mirth ignites, under the beams,
As we weave our whispered dreams.

Together we share in this embrace,
A festival of joy, a wondrous grace.
In the frigid woodland's heart,
The night's embrace plays its part.

Whispers of Winter's Gaze

In the stillness of winter's breath,
Life's magic thrives, warding off death.
Footsteps crunch on a carpet of white,
Each moment holds a spark of delight.

The trees wear coats of frosted lace,
Inviting all to join the chase.
With every gust, the branches sway,
Whispers of winter lead the way.

Laughter echoes in the crisp air,
Friends entwined in warmth and care.
Chasing shadows, we sing aloud,
Festive spirits proud and unbowed.

This season glows, with love in gaze,
Beneath a sky of twinkling rays.
Together we cherish, together we play,
In the whispers of winter's gaze.

Shadows in the Snow

Shadows dance across the field,
As winter's magic is revealed.
Beneath the stars, our spirits rise,
In the silent night, joy never dies.

Footprints trail in the snowy glow,
Mapping laughter in the flow.
With every twirl and joyful cheer,
We celebrate this time of year.

Beneath the moon's enchanting light,
We gather close, hearts shining bright.
Sharing stories, warmth, and song,
Together, we know where we belong.

So let the snowy shadows play,
As we embrace this festive sway.
In every heart, a spark to grow,
Together, we thrive in the snow.

Ghosts in the Snowy Pines

In the woods where shadows play,
Whispers dance on frosty air,
Moonlight kisses snowy blades,
Ghostly figures, bright and rare.

Laughter echoes through the trees,
As the night begins to twirl,
Sparkling in the winter's freeze,
Creating dreams in silver swirl.

Joyful hearts beneath the stars,
Warming hands with hot cocoa,
Mirrored skies, like porcelain jars,
Invite us to share the glow.

In the pines, the secrets keep,
Celebrate the festive mood,
With every cheer, our spirits leap,
Nature sings a joyful brood.

Cloaked by Winter's Embrace

Snowflakes twirl like dancers bright,
All around the world transforms,
Whispers soft, the stars ignite,
Winter's cloak, in beauty warms.

Frosty branches, coated white,
Sparkle under moon's soft gaze,
Children's laughter, pure delight,
Fill the night with love's sweet praise.

Candles flicker, windows glow,
Homes aglow with happiness,
Around the hearth, the warmth will flow,
Bonds of love, we now profess.

Happiness in every heart,
Celebrate this wondrous time,
From this magic, none will part,
Together, we will share the rhyme.

A Frosted Elegy of Night

Silvery moon, a watchful eye,
Over fields of pristine white,
Winds weave tales that sigh and fly,
Beneath the stars, all hearts ignite.

Eager voices fill the air,
Songs of joy, so sweetly sung,
Wrapped in laughter, free from care,
In the glow, we all feel young.

Echoes of the past reside,
In the flurry of the night,
Memories we hold with pride,
In this dance of pure delight.

As the frost claims every shade,
We embrace what life bestows,
In this time, new dreams are made,
In the frost, our spirit grows.

Omens in the Glacial Glow

Lights aglow in winter's breath,
Glistening softly in the night,
Ancient tales of life and death,
In the quiet, pure delight.

Twinkling stars like wishes shared,
Secrets held by frosty trees,
Gifts of love that none have aired,
Whispers carried on the breeze.

Gathering around the fire's light,
Stories woven, hope's embrace,
Celebrating through the night,
In the warmth, we find our place.

As the glacial glow unfolds,
Hearts entwined, we stand as one,
Crafting memories like gold,
In this fest, we all are spun.

Arctic Riddles Unraveled

In the land where the snowflakes dance,
Bright auroras weave their chance.
Laughter echoes through the cold,
Stories of warmth and joy unfold.

Underneath the shimmering skies,
With twinkling stars, the spirit flies.
Smiles abound in the frosty air,
Together we tread without a care.

Ice sculptures glint in twilight's glow,
Fires crackle gently, warming the flow.
With friends around, the night ignites,
Every heart beats with pure delights.

In this realm where the cold is light,
We gather close, a festive sight.
Wonders of winter bring us near,
Riddles of joy, so very clear.

Night's Serene Embrace

As the twilight whispers soft and low,
Moonlight sprinkles a magical glow.
Stars like diamonds wink in the dark,
The world transforms with a twinkling spark.

In this calm, where echoes blend,
Peaceful moments, we can't pretend.
Hot cocoa smiles in frosty mugs,
Sharing stories, and warm heart hugs.

Winter's chill can't freeze our cheer,
Laughter bubbles as friends draw near.
With every breath, we feel the grace,
In the silent beauty of night's embrace.

In shades of blue and shimmering white,
We dance through dreams, a heart's delight.
Together we find our joy tonight,
In the warm glow of starlit flight.

Tracks in the Crystal Realm

Snowflakes fall like whispered dreams,
Covering the earth in sparkling creams.
We stride forth, leaving prints behind,
In the air, pure joy intertwined.

Eager eyes gaze at the wonder,
As the chilly wind plays like thunder.
Nature's canvas, a frosty delight,
Festive pathways glow in moonlight.

Gathering round with hearts so bright,
With laughter echoing into the night.
Building snowmen, creating art,
Each small moment, a treasured part.

In the crystal realm where we play,
Every track leads us on our way.
With each footprint, stories untold,
Festivities bloom as the world unfolds.

A Glimmer in the Frozen Wood

Deep in the forest where silence reigns,
Glistening trails invoke gentle chains.
A glimmer here, a flicker there,
With woodland spirits in festive flare.

Branches twinkling, a joyful sight,
Nature adorned in pure delight.
With every step, the calmness sings,
Embraced by winter and all it brings.

Gathered together, we share a dream,
Hot cider steaming, we laugh and beam.
The frozen wood whispers tales anew,
In the hush of night, our spirits grew.

Among the pines, we find our cheer,
A sanctuary where love is near.
In the heart of winter, friendships bloom,
A glimmer shining through the icy gloom.

Underneath a Crystal Canopy

Underneath a crystal canopy,
Laughter twirls like snowflakes bright,
Joy wraps us in a warm embrace,
As stars play peekaboo with night.

Candles dance with flickering flames,
Whispers of magic fill the air,
We raise our cups to friendship's name,
In hearts, a glowing light we share.

The world is draped in silver dreams,
While joy cascades like gentle streams,
Carols echo through the trees,
Bringing warmth and memories.

Bright baubles twinkle overhead,
With every cheer, new hopes are fed,
Underneath this gleaming show,
The spirit of the season grows.

The Cooled Breath of the Night

The cooled breath of the night descends,
As magic weaves through every sound,
Beneath the moon, the world suspends,
In hushed serenity, joy is found.

Lanterns glowing, casting light,
Each face aglow with borrowed rays,
We gather close, our hearts ignite,
In this cherished moment, we stay.

Laughter bubbles like sparkling wine,
While every hug feels like a song,
In the air, the scent of pine,
A sense of love where we belong.

As frost paints patterns on our skin,
We hold our dreams, embrace the night,
In every smile, a dance begins,
The cooled breath sparks our hearts' delight.

Tales from a Winter's Heart

Tales from a winter's heart unfold,
In whispers wrapped in frosty air,
Stories spun of love and bold,
Where every laugh shows that we care.

Snowflakes gather, soft and bright,
They blanket all with kind delight,
Around the fire, we share our dreams,
Every tale, a bond that gleams.

The warmth of hearth, the glow of cheer,
Brings us close as winter's near,
With cocoa hugs and sweetened treats,
Each moment's magic, life repeats.

From winter's heart, we find our way,
Through tales of joy, we choose to stay,
In every giggle, spark of light,
Our festive spirit takes to flight.

Specters of the Frosted Glen

Specters of the frosted glen arise,
They dance on whispers, soft and sweet,
Mirroring the twinkling skies,
Where every step feels like a treat.

With every footfall, joy awakens,
As laughter blends with shimmering air,
Around us, every spirit beckons,
Inviting us to play and share.

The trees wear coats of icy lace,
While fires crackle, hearts aglow,
Embracing warmth in every space,
With tales of wonder, sweet and slow.

Together, we weave a tapestry,
Of festive cheers and singing joy,
In this glen, our spirits roam free,
Capturing bliss that none can destroy.

Secrets Beneath the Snowdrift

The snowflakes dance in the frosty air,
Whispers of joy, a celebration fair.
Beneath the drifts, secrets they keep,
Silent and soft, as the world falls asleep.

Children's laughter rings out clear,
Bundled in mittens, cheeks rosy with cheer.
Snowmen rise up, with hats held high,
A twinkling love 'neath the winter sky.

In every corner, a story unfolds,
Of warmth and hope in the bitter cold.
Hot cocoa bubbles by fireside's glow,
While dreams take flight in the evening snow.

Whispering Winds in White

Whispers of winter float on the breeze,
Dancing together with the fluttering leaves.
A tapestry woven of white and gold,
Each gust of wind carries tales retold.

The crackling fire paints shadows that play,
As night falls gently, chasing the day.
Bundled in blankets, we gather around,
In the warmth of the glow, true happiness found.

Stars twinkle bright in the velvet expanse,
Inviting us out for a snowy dance.
With laughter and joy, our spirits arise,
In the embrace of winter, our hearts harmonize.

Chasing the Frosted Glimpses

Footprints trail softly in the blanket white,
Chasing frosted glimpses of pure delight.
We twirl and we spin, in the chill of the night,
While lanterns shimmer with warm, gentle light.

Around the old tree, we hang shiny cheer,
Garlands of laughter for all to hear.
Tinsel glistens like stars from above,
Binding our moments with joy and with love.

The world holds its breath, a magical hush,
As snowflakes drift down in a shimmering rush.
With every new flake, the dreams come alive,
In the heart of the night, our spirits will thrive.

Eyes of the Ice-Cloaked Hunter

In the stillness of night, shadows appear,
Eyes of the hunter, glinting with cheer.
Clad in white armor, so fierce yet so bright,
A graceful ballet in the pale moonlight.

With whispers of frost, the landscape gleams,
Each movement a story, woven from dreams.
The secrets of winter, held deep in the snow,
Awaiting the dawn and the light's gentle glow.

Through thickets and trees, the magic unfurls,
In the heart of the wild, where nature swirls.
Together we bask in this winter's embrace,
Finding warmth in the chill, in this frozen space.

Eyes Like Shimmering Stars

In the night sky, they dance so bright,
Glimmers of joy, pure delight.
A warm embrace in the cool night air,
Laughter and love, everywhere.

Crisp laughter rings through the festive cheer,
Celebrations abound, loved ones near.
With every twinkling, hearts take flight,
Under the magic of starlit night.

Candles flicker, shadows play,
Whispers of wishes flutter and sway.
Joyous hearts in radiant glow,
In this moment, happiness flows.

Toasting with friends, spirits high,
In this gathering, we touch the sky.
Eyes like stars, shining so true,
Together in bliss, me and you.

Beneath the Chill of Twilight

As daylight fades into dusk's embrace,
The world transforms with a tender grace.
Colors dance in a vibrant show,
Beneath the chill, warmth starts to flow.

Gathered together, we share our tales,
Under the glow where laughter prevails.
Pumpkin spice and roasted treats,
Echoes of joy in the festive beats.

Fireflies waltz in the evening haze,
Capturing hearts in a shimmering blaze.
Conversations bloom like flowers bright,
In the magic of this twilight night.

Joyful songs drift through the air,
Moments cherished, beyond compare.
Under this sky, with spirits free,
Together we weave our tapestry.

The Silent Stalker's Path

In shadows deep, the night unfolds,
Secrets whisper, stories told.
A journey awaits, silent and bright,
As stars guide the way, a spark in the night.

With careful steps, we wander through,
Cloaked in mystery, the world feels new.
Echoes of laughter in the crisp air,
A festive spirit, everywhere.

Pine-scented air and warm flickers glow,
Celebrations pulse, a rhythmic flow.
Beneath the moon's watchful gaze,
We dance through the night in joyous ways.

Paths intertwined, hearts intertwine,
In this beautiful tale, we draw the line.
With every laugh, and every cheer,
We carve our footprints, year after year.

Isolation in a Crystal Realm

Amidst the stillness, a glittering space,
Fragments of light in a serene embrace.
Crystal reflections sparkle and gleam,
Whispers of magic, an enchanting dream.

Though solitude wraps its gentle shroud,
Silent wonders form a festive crowd.
Echoes of joy drift through the air,
In this crystal realm, beyond compare.

Every shadow holds a spark of grace,
A dance of colors, the smiles they trace.
In this embrace, hearts learn to sing,
In isolation, festive joys take wing.

Through icy pathways, we find our way,
In this crystalline ballet, we sway.
Though apart, we are never alone,
In this sparkling world, we've found a home.

Paws Pressed in the Cold

In a blanket of snow, we dance and play,
Tiny paws leave tracks, a joyous ballet.
Laughter echoes bright in the shimmering light,
Winter's chilly breath feels just right.

Sleds race down hills, hearts drum like a band,
Hot cocoa in hand, friendship so grand.
Frosty air sparkles, each moment's a thrill,
In this festive wonder, time seems to stand still.

Snowflakes like diamonds, twirl in the gloom,
As carols float softly, filling each room.
With family gathered, and spirits so high,
We cherish these moments, as the night draws nigh.

Under stars that twinkle, we gather near,
Each smile like a lantern, lighting our cheer.
With paws pressed in cold, we bridge joy and fun,
In winter's embrace, our hearts are as one.

The Embrace of Winter's Veil

Softly the snow falls, a silken embrace,
Covering the earth in a shimmering lace.
Children in mittens, crafting dreams divine,
With laughter and joy, their spirits align.

The fire crackles warmly, glowing with cheer,
Families gather, with loved ones held dear.
The smell of fresh cookies drifts through the air,
In the heart of winter, there's magic to share.

Icicles hanging, like chandeliers bright,
Shimmering softly in the deep winter night.
With every warm hug, and each festive song,
The embrace of winter wraps us all along.

As carolers gather, their voices take flight,
Spreading the joy in the stillness of night.
In this wondrous season, where love will prevail,
We find warmth and kindness in winter's soft veil.

Reflections Off a Frosty Glass

Raindrops freeze softly on windows so clear,
Creating a canvas for laughter and cheer.
Each breath is a whisper, a frosty delight,
As the world outside sparkles, pure and bright.

Inside we gather, with stories to share,
Hot chocolate warming our hearts in the air.
With friends all around, our worries dissolve,
In reflections of joy, our lives intertwine, evolve.

The glow of the fireplace throws shadows that dance,
As we laugh and we sing, lost in a trance.
The beauty of winter, a magical sight,
Creating a canvas filled with pure light.

Through reflections we see, the love and the grace,
Of festive gatherings, each smile a warm embrace.
With frost on the glass, and warmth in our hearts,
We treasure these moments, where the magic starts.

Glittering Veils of Mystery

Bells are ringing through the night,
Laughter dances, hearts take flight.
Under strings of twinkling stars,
We celebrate, no more scars.

Candles flicker, shadows play,
Magic weaves in bright array.
Joyful whispers fill the air,
Moments cherished, memories rare.

Colors swirl like dreams untold,
Stories shared, a warmth to hold.
In the glow of love's embrace,
Every smile finds its place.

Toast to life, to love, to cheer,
Together we will conquer fear.
In glittering veils, our hearts unite,
A festive night, pure delight.

Shadows Under the Polar Moon

Ice crystals glimmer, pure and bright,
Underneath the polar light.
Footsteps crunch, a lively tune,
Magic whispers, shadows croon.

Fires crackle, warmth inside,
Snowflakes twirl, a joyful ride.
Gather 'round, let stories flow,
In the moonlight, spirits glow.

Sleds racing with gleeful shouts,
Winter's spirit, no doubts.
With every laugh, we cast away,
Frosty thoughts, come what may.

Under stars, wrapped in light,
Together, we embrace the night.
In shadows soft, friendship's bloom,
Shines bright under the polar moon.

In the Realm of Frosted Dreams

Winds whisper secrets, soft and clear,
In frosted fields, we gather near.
Snowman smiles, a child's delight,
In this realm, everything's bright.

Glowing lanterns light the scene,
Wonders paint the world serene.
Carols glide through the chilly air,
Each note a treasure, beyond compare.

Hot cocoa brews, warmth in our hands,
Together building fanciful lands.
Dreams take flight on winter's breeze,
Heartfelt laughter aims to please.

In this realm, where joy resides,
Magic flows like the ocean tides.
Frosted dreams, we hold so dear,
Together always, year after year.

Frosted Gaze of Nature's Guardian

A silver blanket hugs the ground,
Nature's guardian all around.
Trees wear coats of sparkling white,
In the hush of the festive night.

Branches bow beneath the weight,
Frosted beauty, delicate fate.
Whispers float like feathers tossed,
In this wonder, none are lost.

Crimson berries, bright against snow,
Life persists in the cold below.
Creating joy in every glance,
In nature's beauty, we find our chance.

Gather 'round, let spirits soar,
For in this magic, we crave more.
Nature's guardian holds us tight,
Frosted gaze, a pure delight.

A Murmured Tale of Ice

In the glimmering night, laughter swells,
As whispers of joy weave magical spells.
Snowflakes dance like stars in the air,
Beneath the moon's charm, hearts freely share.

Candles flicker in the brisk, cold air,
Each light a promise, a joy to declare.
Children's laughter rings through the trees,
As frost-kissed dreams sway with the breeze.

Footprints imprinted on soft, white ground,
Echoes of merriment, warmth all around.
The air is alive with stories untold,
Wrapped in the shimmer of silver and gold.

So gather 'round, let the music caress,
In this tale of ice, let our souls express.
With every heartbeat, let the night glow,
For in this festive tale, love overflows.

Beneath Frost's Ethereal Glow

Beneath the heavens, in a blanket of white,
Frost paints the world in shimmering light.
Chimneys puffing warm dreams into the sky,
As the spirit of winter whispers a sigh.

Laughter erupts from the corners of trees,
Chasing the chill with a warm, gentle breeze.
Lights twinkle like fireflies caught in a net,
In this frozen wonderland, joy's not to forget.

With mugs steaming rich, we gather to toast,
To friends and to family, the ones we love most.
The stars nod above in their silvery gowns,
Beneath frost's glow, no one wears frowns.

So let us embrace this sweet, fleeting time,
With stories and songs, in rhythm and rhyme.
As snowflakes drift softly, and daylight departs,
We celebrate winter, uniting our hearts.

Walks of the Winter Spirit

In the quiet of dusk, when the sun starts to fade,
Winter's spirit walks through the twilight cascade.
Footsteps are soft, muffled by snow,
Each step a dance, as the cold winds blow.

With each breath released, a small cloud of mist,
The warmth of our laughter can hardly be missed.
Branches hold treasures, a glistening show,
Of crystals that sparkle like stars hung low.

The night wraps us warmly in layers of cheer,
As we wander through dreams, with our loved ones near.
Whispers of magic drift through the trees,
With joy in our hearts and a chill in the breeze.

So let's hold the moments, create and sustain,
In the walks of the winter, let love be our gain.
Together we'll wander, beneath the moon's light,
Our spirits entwined in the stillness of night.

The Frozen Gaze of Midnight

The clock strikes twelve, the world holds its breath,
In the frozen gaze, we dance with sweet depth.
Stars gather closely as if to preside,
Over moments of magic we'll cherish with pride.

Each corner aglow with the warmth of our fires,
As stories unfold, fulfilling our desires.
Frosted trees shimmer like guardians bold,
Embracing our laughter, our secrets retold.

With echoes of joy flowing soft through the night,
We cherish each second, wrapped in delight.
The air filled with music, a tuneful embrace,
In the frozen gaze of midnight, we find our place.

Let the night linger long, let our hearts sing,
In this magical season, we'll celebrate spring.
For every cold moment is woven with grace,
In the dance of the winter, our spirits will trace.

Chilling Elegance of the Night

Under the stars, the world is aglow,
Laughter rings out, the warmth starts to flow.
With every heartbeat, the joy takes its flight,
In the chilling elegance of this magical night.

Candles are flickering, casting soft light,
Friends gather close, holding futures so bright.
Snowflakes like whispers twirl down from above,
Wrapped in the spirit of warmth and of love.

Echoes of music dance freely through air,
Feet tap to rhythms that lighten the care.
With sparkling mugs raised, we toast to delight,
In this chilling elegance, our hearts feel so right.

The night stretches onward, a blanket divine,
Every shared story, a glimmer, a sign.
In laughter and joy, we embrace what is right,
In the chilling elegance of this magical night.

Secrets of the Frosted Forest

Whispers of snowflakes float through the air,
Secrets of the forest, a beauty so rare.
Trees dressed in shimmer, pure elegance calls,
Nature's own magic from the heavens falls.

Moonlight cascades on a silvery stream,
Frosted reflections, like a peaceful dream.
The silence envelops, a hush that brings peace,
In the secrets of the forest, all worries cease.

Beneath the great pines, we tread soft and light,
Each step in wonder, a holiday sight.
With laughter and joy, our spirits take flight,
In the peaceful embrace of the frosted night.

Gathered together, we share tales anew,
In this frosted haven, where friendships grew.
The secrets we hold, like treasures ignite,
In the heart of the forest, so warm and so bright.

The Moonlit Hunter

In shadows he prowls, under soft silver light,
The moonlit hunter, a figure of night.
With grace in his movement, he knows every path,
A master of silence, he dances with wrath.

The forest awakens, a stage set for show,
Creatures are stirring, the air filled with glow.
In every small rustle, his senses delight,
The thrill of the chase on this magical night.

Stars twinkle brightly, as if holding their breath,
For the dance of the hunter, a rhythm with death.
With instincts ignited, a legend takes flight,
In the heart of the woodland, under soft moonlight.

And as dawn approaches, the chase will still linger,
His tales of the night, like threads on a finger.
The moonlit hunter returns from his plight,
To the secrets of shadows that veil the daylight.

Shimmering Frost on Silent Paths

Morning greets softly, a tapestry spun,
With shimmering frost, a new day begun.
Paths bid us welcome, each step a delight,
In the sparkle of winter, everything's bright.

Children are laughing, their joy takes to flight,
With snowballs a-flying, they play in pure light.
A chill in the air, yet hearts feel so warm,
As we wander together, embraced by the charm.

The trees wear their coats, a frosted embrace,
While nature rejoices, adorned for our grace.
With whispers of magic, the landscape imbues,
Shimmering frost dances on each step we choose.

Amongst the stillness, a beauty divine,
We capture the moments, in laughter we shine.
With shimmering paths that beckon our pace,
In the world of the frost, we find our true place.

The Stillness of Frozen Echoes

In the air, a laughter sings,
Whispers of joy in icy rings.
Snowflakes dance in the soft light,
Echoing magic through the night.

Fires crackle, warmth surrounds,
Glowing hearts in merry sounds.
Families gather, stories shared,
In this moment, love is bared.

Starlit skies, a blanket rare,
Enchanting smiles, the evening fair.
Every heartbeat, a festive tune,
Underneath the silvery moon.

With hands held tight, we embrace,
Together in this happy space.
Frozen echoes softly blend,
In the stillness, joy won't end.

Treasures Hidden in Snow

Underneath the frosty field,
Magic lies, a mystery sealed.
Glistening diamonds beneath bright skies,
Nature's bounty, a sweet surprise.

Children laugh, their spirits high,
Building castles, reaching the sky.
Every snowball, a cherished fight,
In the soft glow of winter light.

Footprints trace a joyful path,
Every echo bursts with laughter's wrath.
Treasures hidden in every flake,
Memories woven, a life we make.

Evening falls, the stories grow,
Under stars, the glittering show.
Wrapped in warmth, side by side,
In this season, love is wide.

Shadows of Silence in Icebound Woods

In the hush of frosted trees,
Whispers float on a gentle breeze.
Silent paths where shadows play,
Guarding secrets of the day.

The moon casts a soft, silver glow,
Painting landscapes of pure snow.
Footsteps crunched, a joyful sound,
In these woods, happiness is found.

Branches laden, sparkling bright,
Stars above in a blanket of night.
Every shadow holds a tale,
In this stillness, spirits sail.

Gather close, feel the cheer,
Together, we have nothing to fear.
In the silence, our dreams ignite,
In icebound woods, pure delight.

Secrets in the Frosted Dawn

Morning breaks with a jeweled crown,
Awakening whispers all around.
Frosted breath on windows clear,
A new day's promise, festive cheer.

Colors bloom in the crisp, cold air,
Nature's beauty everywhere.
Snow-kissed trees in shimmering light,
Reveal the secrets hidden tight.

Children chase in a world so bright,
Building dreams with pure delight.
Every snowman, a joyful sight,
In the dawning morning light.

Together we share this sacred space,
Laughter echoes, love's embrace.
In each glimmer, moments found,
Secrets live in the frosted dawn.

The Frosted Haven's Secret

Whispers of joy in the frosty night,
Candles aglow, a warm, soft light.
Laughter and cheer, the snowflakes twirl,
In this haven, our hearts unfurl.

Sweet treats abound on the table laid,
With stories shared, and memories made.
The scent of pine drifts through the air,
Creating a magic beyond compare.

Children's laughter dances on the breeze,
As frost-kissed branches sway with ease.
Under the moon, secrets are spun,
In this frosted haven, we are one.

Join hands in joy, let the music play,
As we celebrate this festive day.
In the frost and cheer, our spirits soar,
Finding the secrets we all adore.

Silent Dance of Ice and Snow

In the hush, the world is still,
Blanketed soft as the night grows chill.
Snowflakes waltz in a close embrace,
Silent dance of nature's grace.

Glittering stars in the velvet sky,
Whispering wishes as they float by.
The cool air sparkles, crisp and bright,
Creating a spell on this festive night.

Paths are etched in the glistening white,
With laughter echoing, pure delight.
Hot cocoa warms our cheerful hands,
As joy unfolds in this winterland.

Fires crackle, stories unfold,
In this moment, warmth over cold.
Together we sing, together we share,
In this silent dance, love fills the air.

Haunting Melody of Winter's Call

The wind whispers songs of frosty lore,
Echoing dreams from the days of yore.
With every flake that graces the ground,
A haunting melody, a sweet, soft sound.

Trees embrace their winter coats,
While shadows sway like spectral boats.
In the stillness, a spirit calls,
Inviting us to these winter halls.

Footprints lead us on snowy trails,
Where laughter peals and joy prevails.
Each note of winter is pure and clear,
As we gather 'round with those we hold dear.

Under the twilight, we make our stand,
With hearts in tune, hand in hand.
A melody swells, our voices rise,
In winter's embrace, our spirit flies.

Beneath Stars and Snowflakes

Beneath the stars, where secrets lie,
Snowflakes fall like a soft lullaby.
Gathered 'round, we share our dreams,
In this wonderland, joy brightly gleams.

Twinkling lights adorn the trees,
Dancing gently in the winter breeze.
Laughter sparkles, an endless tune,
As we chase the magic of the moon.

With every glance, the night unfolds,
Stories of hope and love retold.
Fires crackle, warm and bright,
In the heart of winter's delight.

So let us cherish the moments we share,
With festive hearts and love laid bare.
In this winter's embrace, forever we'll stay,
Beneath stars and snowflakes, come what may.

Enigma of the Frosted Forest

In the heart of winter's glow,
The frosted trees put on a show.
Whispers dance on icy air,
Magic floats without a care.

Snowflakes twirl, a playful flight,
Sparkling diamonds, pure delight.
Laughter echoes, warm and bright,
In the forest clad in white.

Nature dons her frosty crown,
A joyful spirit all around.
Each branch bows low with grace and charm,
Wrapped softly in winter's warm.

So gather 'round, let hearts unite,
In this enchanted, snowy night.
Where every step a tale unfurls,
In the magic of the frosted worlds.

Beneath the Whispering Pines

Beneath the pines where laughter grows,
A realm of cheer, where friendship flows.
The sunbeams dance through boughs above,
A blessing wrapped in nature's love.

Footsteps crunch on a carpet white,
Each moment filled with pure delight.
Fires crackle, tales ignite,
As stars emerge in twinkling sight.

A tapestry of joy is spun,
Beneath the pines, where hearts are one.
With every sip of warming cheer,
The spirit thrives; we hold it dear.

And as the night draws close and deep,
We weave our hopes, our dreams to keep.
In every whisper, every sigh,
Beneath the pines, our souls can fly.

Cold Elegance in the Wild

A shimmering veil on the rugged ground,
Cold elegance in nature found.
Each frosty breath a jeweled trace,
In the wild, we find our place.

Icicles hang like chandeliers,
Glistening bright as winter nears.
With every step, the world transforms,
In a dance that easily warms.

The crisp air sings a joyous tune,
Underneath the silver moon.
With laughter shared and spirits high,
Cold elegance will never die.

So let us revel in this bliss,
A fleeting moment not to miss.
For in this wild, so bold and bright,
We find our joy on winter's night.

The Last Trail of Winter

On the last trail where snowflakes play,
Winter bids us farewell today.
With vibrant hues the world ignite,
As spring approaches, pure and bright.

The sun dips low, a golden blaze,
We dance through time, in winter's gaze.
Each step we take, the magic swells,
In the stories of our hearts it dwells.

The air is crisp, the laughter flows,
As nature's beauty gently glows.
With every moment, joy's embrace,
The last trail of winter leaves a trace.

So let us cherish all that's gone,
The memories linger, softly drawn.
In the twilight, we raise a cheer,
For the last trail of winter near.

Frozen Echoes in Twilight

In twilight's dance, the snowflakes play,
With laughter bright, they drift away.
The world ignites in shimmering hues,
As joy unfolds in frosty views.

Each echo sweet in winter's hold,
A tapestry of dreams retold.
The chill embraces hearts so warm,
In frozen echoes, love takes form.

With every twirl, the stars align,
A festive spirit, pure divine.
Underneath the moon's soft gaze,
We celebrate in winter's blaze.

So raise a glass to frosty nights,
In frozen echoes, pure delights.
With friends around and spirits high,
This twilight magic lifts us high.

Silence of the Silver Gleam

In silent nights where silver gleams,
The world awakes from hushed, soft dreams.
With gentle whispers, snowflakes fall,
A festive hush enchants us all.

The moonlight dances on the snow,
As laughter sparkles, warm and slow.
With every twinkle, joy ignites,
In silver silence, pure delights.

The trees wear gowns of icy lace,
As hearts embrace this frosty space.
With friends beside, we share the cheer,
In harmony throughout the year.

So let the silver gleam shine bright,
In festive calm, our spirits light.
We raise our voices, singing clear,
In silence sweet, we hold what's dear.

The Hidden Hunter's Serenade

Beneath the stars, the hunter sighs,
Through whispered woods, his laughter flies.
With every shadow, tales unfold,
A serenade in night so cold.

He wanders deep where secrets weave,
Amidst the pines, the heart believes.
A festive song, the night will sing,
As nature's pulse begins to spring.

With every note, the earth awakes,
In haunting tunes, the silence breaks.
The hidden joys in twilight glade,
Illuminate the path he's made.

So gather round, hear nature's call,
In harmony, we rise and fall.
The hunter's serenade, so true,
A festive heart in all we do.

Beneath the Glacial Canopy

Beneath the glacial canopy wide,
Where icy branches gently glide.
The world beneath, in peace, does bloom,
In festive shades, dispelling gloom.

With every flake that drifts and sways,
The charm of winter brightly plays.
A joyous heart, a laughter shared,
In glacial light, all souls are bared.

The crispness fills the evening air,
In every breath, a magic rare.
As sparkling lights reflect the stars,
In frozen dreams, we've come so far.

So dance beneath the glacial night,
With every step, our spirits bright.
We celebrate this wondrous time,
In jubilant rhythm, hearts in rhyme.

Whispers of Winter Paws

In the glow of the evening light,
Soft paw prints dance in the snow.
Laughter rings through the crisp air,
As our hearts begin to glow.

Candles flicker, warm and bright,
With a breeze, the spirits soar.
Joyous songs fill the night,
As we gather, evermore.

Snowflakes whirl like playful dreams,
Cocoa warms our chilly hands.
Wrapped in blankets, laughter streams,
A festive cheer that never ends.

Underneath the starlit sky,
We share tales of joy and glee.
With winter's magic, we fly,
In this bliss, forever free.

Veils of Silent Snow

Gentle whispers fill the air,
Snowflakes fall like silken lace.
Children's laughter everywhere,
Their joy, a warm embrace.

Twinkling lights adorn the trees,
As carols blend with the chill.
The world slows down with such ease,
Creating memories to thrill.

Hot cider brews, the fire glows,
Embers dance in the night sky.
Sharing stories as it snows,
Underneath the watchful eye.

With each moment, magic grows,
Spreading cheer both far and near.
A festive spirit gently flows,
In the warmth, we hold so dear.

Shadows in Frosted Woods

In the thick of frosty nights,
Underneath the moonlit glow.
Nature whispers sweet delights,
As the stars begin to show.

Footsteps crunch on snow so pure,
Echoes dance through trees so tall.
In this moment, we are sure,
Festive joy will never fall.

Pine scents drift upon the breeze,
Candles flicker in the dark.
Wonders hide amongst the leaves,
As laughter sparks a joyful spark.

Frosty shadows stretch and weave,
As we raise our voice in song.
In this magic, we believe,
Together, we are always strong.

Echoes of Arctic Secrets

In the heart of the Arctic chill,
Echoes whisper tales of yore.
Each step with wonder, each thrill,
In this land, forevermore.

Icicles shimmer like bright jewels,
Underneath the aurora's dance.
Nature's beauty breaks the rules,
Capturing every fleeting chance.

We gather 'round the fire's glow,
Sharing dreams and laughter's song.
With every twinkle, love will grow,
In the warmth where we belong.

Secrets wrapped in winter's fold,
Tell of joy and sweet delight.
In our hearts, these tales are gold,
Beneath the stars, we unite.

Nightfall in a White Drape

The stars twinkle brightly in the dark,
Snowflakes drift gently, leaving their mark.
Laughter and joy dance through the air,
Festive moments, a spell we share.

Candles flicker, their glow so warm,
Families gather, a cozy charm.
Songs of the season rise up with cheer,
A time of love, together we're here.

Glimmers of silver adorn the trees,
Whispers of magic carried by the breeze.
Snow-clad rooftops glisten and shine,
In this winter wonderland, all is divine.

The world transforms under a shimmering veil,
With every heartbeat, our spirits sail.
In the twilight, our dreams take flight,
As nightfall whispers, everything feels right.

Dance of the Winter Shadows

Under blankets of snow so pure,
Winter's embrace feels safe and sure.
The twinkling lights weave tales of old,
In this festive scene, our hearts unfold.

Frosted windows frame joy inside,
Neighbors come close, with laughter we bide.
The echo of music, a soft serenade,
Each note a promise that never will fade.

Sculpted snowmen, all grins and glee,
Children's laughter rang like melody.
With every twirl, shadows dance and sway,
In the warm glow of this winter's ballet.

As stars witness the magic, we unite,
Celebrations bloom beneath the moonlight.
In these moments, true love does flow,
An evening of joy, like the softest snow.

Glint of the Cold Moon

The night sky wears a shimmering crown,
As the cold moon rises, casting down.
With every glance, it holds our gaze,
In this festive night, we're lost in a haze.

The air is crisp, filled with delight,
Lanterns are glowing, a beautiful sight.
Families gather, warmth all around,
In the heart of winter, true love is found.

Echoes of laughter float on the breeze,
While frost-kissed branches sway with ease.
We dance under stars, hearts full of grace,
Each moment cherished, in this sacred space.

With each sparkling glint on the snow,
The magic of winter continues to flow.
Together we celebrate, always to stay,
In the glint of the cold moon, love leads the way.

Amidst Shadows and Snow

In the hush of night, shadows take flight,
Amidst drifts of snow, there's pure delight.
Colorful lights peek through the dark,
A festival spirit ignites a spark.

Songs weave through the silent air,
Voices united, a joyous affair.
The warmth of togetherness, hearts intertwine,
In the glow of the season, our spirits align.

Candied treats and laughter abound,
Magic of winter, in memory found.
Under the starlit texture so rare,
We find our solace, floating on air.

In shadows and snow, we embrace the night,
With every heartbeat, the world feels right.
Together we shine, as bright as the sun,
In this festive wonder, we are all one.

Silent Pawprints in Ice

In the morning light, bright and clear,
Silent pawprints whisper near,
Dancing shadows, soft and light,
Celebrate the frosty night.

Laughter echoes through the trees,
Carried gently by the breeze,
Joyful spirits, hearts so bright,
In this wonder, pure delight.

Snowflakes twirl, a sparkling show,
Blanket white on earth below,
Winter's magic fills the air,
Silent joy is everywhere.

Gather close, let warmth ignite,
Shared tales under stars so bright,
With each step, our hearts are free,
In the frost, sweet harmony.

Glacial Secrets Unfurled

Underneath the icy sheen,
Glacial secrets, serene and keen,
Twinkling lights on frozen streams,
A world awash in snowy dreams.

Whispers of the winter's lore,
In the silence, we explore,
Each breath a plume, crisp and clear,
Moments linger, warm and dear.

Ice crystals dance, a brilliant sight,
In the glow of winter's night,
Festive cheer fills every space,
Joyful laughter, warm embrace.

As the stars begin to gleam,
We celebrate, we laugh, we dream,
In this wonderland so grand,
Together, hand in hand.

Echoes of a Frosted Wild

In the forest, quiet and bright,
Echoes of the frosted night,
Nature's canvas, white and bold,
Stories of the winter told.

Softly gliding, shadows play,
In the snow, our spirits sway,
Hoar frost glimmers, fresh and new,
A symphony of silver hue.

With each flake, a dance so free,
Winter's joy, a jubilee,
Footprints form a fleeting trace,
Memories in this frozen space.

Gather 'round, the warmth we share,
Through the chill, we breathe the air,
In this wild, a heart so bright,
Echoes weave through the night.

Beneath the Frosty Veil

Beneath the frost, the world awakes,
Silent beauty, stillness makes,
Shimmering in the dawn's soft glow,
A festive pulse, a gentle flow.

Boughs adorned with snowy lace,
Nature's charm, a warm embrace,
Crisp air carries laughter's call,
As we revel, one and all.

With every step, the magic grows,
In this realm where kindness flows,
Hearts unite in joy's refrain,
Underneath the falling rain.

Celebrate the chill, the light,
Find your joy in winter's night,
Together, in this frosty tale,
We dance beneath the frosty veil.

The Serpent's Winter Song

A serpent glides on glittered ground,
With scales like stars where dreams abound.
Its song a whisper, soft and light,
Dancing shadows in the night.

Beneath the moon's warm, loving gaze,
It weaves through trees in frosty haze.
Laughter echoes, joy in the air,
A festive spirit everywhere.

Snowflakes twirl like confetti bright,
In a world where hearts take flight.
Each note a spark, alive and free,
A celebration of harmony.

With each breath, the chill is sweet,
As warmth and merriment compete.
Together, we sing of love and cheer,
Embracing winter, drawing near.

In the Depths of Frosty Silence

In stillness deep, the world is white,
Frosty silence cloaked in night.
Stars above like candy bright,
Twinkling softly, pure delight.

We gather close, wrapped in dreams,
Around the fire, bright it seems.
Laughter bubbles, stories shared,
Hearts are open, loved and cared.

Shadows dance on icy ground,
Whispers of joy all around.
In every heart, a festive cheer,
As winter's magic draws us near.

Snowflakes gather without a sound,
Coating all that can be found.
In frosty silence, love ignites,
Festive warmth in winter nights.

Echoes of Snow-Covered Paths

Footprints traced on snow's embrace,
Whispers linger, timeless grace.
Every step a joyful dance,
In this season, hearts advance.

Children's laughter fills the air,
Chasing moments, pure and rare.
Echoes of joy on winter's trails,
Each sound a song that never fails.

Underneath the branches bare,
Magic twinkles everywhere.
In the hush, a story told,
Of festive days, bright and bold.

As twilight casts its silken veil,
Frosty breath weaves a fairy tale.
Together, we rejoice and sing,
In winter's arms, the joy we bring.

An Outline Against the Silvered Sky

A silhouette as night draws near,
Outlined stark against the clear.
The silver dust upon the land,
A festive canvas, pure and grand.

With every twinkle, dreams ignite,
Stars align in the quiet night.
Nature's beauty, dressed in white,
We celebrate this wondrous sight.

Candles flicker, warmth inside,
Chasing shadows, joy is wide.
Linking hearts in the twilight,
Filling souls with pure delight.

The outline fades as laughter grows,
In winter's breath, love overflows.
In this moment, we belong,
Together singing life's sweet song.

Crystal Pawprints at Dusk

In twilight glow, the pawprints gleam,
Flickering lights in a frosty dream.
Joyful laughter fills the air,
As snowflakes dance without a care.

Warm fires crackle, stories unfold,
Whispers of wonder, festive and bold.
Each pawprint tells of joy today,
In a world where magic finds its way.

Children chase shadows, hearts full of cheer,
Snowmen stand tall, the season draws near.
With every step in this icy delight,
We celebrate life on this starry night.

Underneath stars, the world feels alive,
Crystal pawprints where dreams can thrive.
Gathering moments, a treasure to keep,
In memories woven, our spirits leap.

Surrounded by Frosty Silence

Whispers of winter, peaceful and still,
The world draped in snow, a gentle chill.
Each flake a secret, soft in its fall,
Echoes of silence, a magical call.

Beneath the moonlight, shadows entwine,
Frosty branches in grand design.
Laughter rings out like bells in the night,
In this frosty silence, hearts feel so light.

Sparkling shimmers on fields of white,
Firesides glow, a warm, cozy sight.
Hot cocoa steaming, lips curled in smiles,
Frosty silence wraps us for miles.

Together we gather, stories to share,
Memories made in the cold evening air.
In frosty tranquility, magic takes flight,
Surrounded by silence, our hearts feel so bright.

The Frozen Eyes Within

Glittering frost on windows so clear,
Reflecting laughter, warmth drawing near.
In frozen eyes, we glimpse the night,
Whispers of dreams take sudden flight.

Candles flicker with golden light,
Glances exchanged, a heartwarming sight.
In every twinkle, a story unfolds,
The magic of winter, timeless and bold.

Festive melodies dance through the air,
Frosted whispers, secrets to share.
In the frozen depths, a fire ignites,
Uniting our spirits on these joyful nights.

Hope shines brighter than the stars above,
In frozen eyes, we find all our love.
Each moment cherished, each heartbeat a gift,
In this winter wonder, our souls start to lift.

Veils of Ice and Mystery

Through veils of ice, the shadows wane,
Discovering magic in frosty terrain.
The world glimmers under the moon's soft gaze,
In mystery wrapped, we lose ourselves in praise.

Footsteps crunch on the blanket of white,
Embracing each moment, pure and bright.
Nature holds secrets in every snowdrift,
A festive wonder, a heartfelt gift.

Sparkling crystals adorn every tree,
Silent enchantment, wild and free.
With every breath, winter's story is told,
With laughter and joy, our hearts uncontrolled.

In veils of ice, our dreams intertwine,
Creating a tapestry, joyous, divine.
As we wander through this season's embrace,
In the heart of the frost, we find our place.

Twilight in the Frozen Land

In twilight's glow, the snowflakes dance,
Colorful lights in a winter's romance.
Joyful laughter fills the chilly air,
A festive spirit, beyond compare.

Families gather, hearts all aglow,
Creating memories in the soft, white snow.
Warmth of fire and cocoa in hand,
Together we shine in this frozen land.

Silent Songs of the Frozen Pines

Whispers of winter through the tall pines,
Silent songs of joy, where the sun shines.
Snow-covered branches, a beautiful sight,
Harmonies linger in the calm of night.

Beneath the moon, a soft silver glow,
Carefree spirits drift, like the falling snow.
Glimmers of starlight spark joy and delight,
In this stillness, the world feels so bright.

Lurking in Stillness

In the woods so quiet, where shadows play,
Festive spirits dance in a frosty ballet.
Under the cover of a starlit sky,
Echoes of laughter softly float by.

A hint of mischief in the crisp, cold air,
Whispers of secrets that we gladly share.
With every heartbeat, we feel the thrill,
Magic of winter, a wondrous chill.

Murmurs of the Icy Woods

The icy woods weave tales of delight,
Murmurs of joy beneath the soft light.
Cardinals flit through the branches so bare,
Draped in white, their beauty to share.

Together we wander, hearts intertwined,
Lost in the magic our spirits find.
A chorus of cheer fills the frosty space,
In the snowy embrace, we leave our trace.

www.ingramcontent.com/pod-product-compliance
Lightning Source LLC
LaVergne TN
LVHW011317050125
800448LV00003B/178